T0025888

Learning to Read, Step by Step!

Ready to Read Preschool–Kindergarten
• big type and easy words • rhyme and rhythm • picture clues
For children who know the alphabet and are eager to
begin reading.

Reading with Help Preschool–Grade 1
• basic vocabulary • short sentences • simple stories
For children who recognize familiar words and sound out
new words with help.

Reading on Your Own Grades 1–3
• engaging characters • easy-to-follow plots • popular topics
For children who are ready to read on their own.

Reading Paragraphs Grades 2–3
• challenging vocabulary • short paragraphs • exciting stories
For newly independent readers who read simple sentences
with confidence.

Ready for Chapters Grades 2–4
• chapters • longer paragraphs • full-color art
For children who want to take the plunge into chapter books
but still like colorful pictures.

STEP INTO READING® is designed to give every child a successful
reading experience. The grade levels are only guides; children will progress
through the steps at their own speed, developing confidence in their reading.
The F&P Text Level on the back cover serves as another tool to help you
choose the right book for your child.

Remember, a lifetime love of reading starts with a single step!

For Margaret Rose
—S.C.

For Karim,
with my deepest gratitude for being there
for me as teacher, friend, and inspiration
—N.T.

Text copyright © 2016 by Suzy Capozzi
Illustrations copyright © 2016 by Nicole Tadgell
Photograph credits: cover © David Turnley/Corbis; p. 47: Peter Turnley/Corbis; p. 48: AP Images/ Themba Hadebe, POOL.

Visit us on the Web!
randomhousekids.com
StepIntoReading.com

Educators and librarians, for a variety of teaching tools, visit us at RHTeachersLibrarians.com

Library of Congress Cataloging-in-Publication Data
Capozzi, Suzy, author.
Nelson Mandela : from prisoner to president / by Suzy Capozzi ; illustrations by Nicole Tadgell. — First edition.
pages cm. — (Step into reading. Step 4)
ISBN 978-0-553-51343-1 (trade pbk.) — ISBN 978-0-375-97467-0 (hardcover library binding) — ISBN 978-0-553-51344-8 (ebook)
1. Mandela, Nelson, 1918–2013—Juvenile literature. 2. Presidents—South Africa—Biography— Juvenile literature. 3. Political prisoners—South Africa—Biography—Juvenile literature. I. Tadgell, Nicole, illustrator. II. Title.
DT1974.C365 2016 968.06'5092—dc23 [B] 2015029519

Printed in the United States of America
10 9 8 7 6 5 4 3 2 1
First Edition

This book has been officially leveled by using the F&P Text Level Gradient™ Leveling System.

STEP INTO READING®

4

STEP
READING PARAGRAPHS

A BIOGRAPHY READER

NELSON MANDELA

From Prisoner to President

by Suzy Capozzi

illustrations by Nicole Tadgell

Random House 🏠 New York

1
President Mandela

MAY 10, 1994. PRETORIA, SOUTH AFRICA.
The sun shines brightly on the crowd
gathered outside the government's offices.
Leaders from all over the world—princes
and presidents—are here to celebrate with
the people. A man walks onto the stage.
The crowd stands and cheers. Nelson
Mandela is here.

Four years ago, Mandela was in jail.
Two weeks ago, he voted for the first time
ever. Today, he will become president!

Mandela raises his right hand and
promises to lead his country. At the age
of seventy-five, he is sworn in as the first
black president of South Africa.

President Mandela speaks to the crowd about the past. For hundreds of years, South Africa was ruled by white people. Their laws strictly limited the rights and opportunities of anyone who was not white. Mandela thanks everyone who helped change the laws and made sure *every* South African could vote.

All day long, President Mandela
thinks about South Africa's history, its
bright future, and his place in it. He
remembers the people who came before
him. He is amazed by everything they did
to make this day happen. "Let there be
justice for all. Let there be peace for all,"
he declares.

2
Tree Shaker

Nelson Mandela was born on July 18, 1918, in the village of Mvezo (mu-VAY-zoh). His birth name, Rolihlahla (KHOH-lee-KLAH-klah), means "tree shaker" or "troublemaker" in Xhosa (KAW-suh). Many South African tribes, like his, speak this language.

His father, Henry, had an important job in the Thembu (TEM-boo) tribe. He counseled the tribe's ruler. But when Rolihlahla was still a baby, his father got into trouble for refusing to obey a white official. The government took away his job and property.

Rolihlahla and his mother had to live

with her family in another village, twenty
miles away. In time, he learned to fish
and to herd sheep and cows, and he
played with the other children. He loved
his new home.

When Rolihlahla was seven, his parents
sent him away to school. This was a great
privilege. The school was run by European
missionaries. On the first day, his teacher
gave him the English name Nelson.

When Nelson was twelve, his father died. Heartbroken, Nelson went to live with the chief of the Thembu tribe. Nelson's father had been the chief's great advisor, and the chief wanted to honor their friendship. He would make sure Nelson received the best education. His home was bigger than any Nelson had ever seen! Nelson played with the chief's children and worked hard at school. Soon he felt at home.

Nelson loved listening to the chief
and his council. Sometimes they told
stories about their people's history. They
also shared problems affecting the tribe.
The chief listened to everyone, whether
they were worried about crops or about
new laws forced on them by the white

government. He decided what was best for the tribe after everyone had a chance to speak. Nelson saw how to lead people by listening.

When he was fifteen, Nelson went to boarding school. His good grades there helped him get accepted to college in 1938.

3
Runaway

At college, Nelson studied and kept busy. He played soccer and acted in plays.

Toward the end of his second year, the students decided they did not like how they were being treated. Nelson joined their protest. The principal said he would not be invited back if he continued to stir up trouble. Nelson left school. But he had an even bigger problem waiting at home. The chief had picked a bride for Nelson! He did not want to marry, so he ran away to a city called Johannesburg.

In 1941, the city offered great opportunities if you were white. But for black people, it was a different story. They had to follow strict laws that limited where they could go and what they could own. Nelson could not keep a job. He was running out of money and choices. Luckily, he became friends with Walter Sisulu. Walter owned a real-estate business helping black South Africans find places to live. He was also involved in the African National Congress (ANC). The ANC wanted black South Africans to have the same rights as white South Africans.

Walter helped Nelson get a job as a law clerk and find a place to live. The next few years flew by. Nelson returned to school and joined the ANC. He started to study the law. Somehow Nelson found time to get married and start a family.

4
Apartness

In 1948, another white political party came into power. They called themselves the National Party, yet white people were a small minority of the whole population. This party wanted to separate the races of South Africa. When they won the election, that is exactly what they did.

After the National Party took control, they passed a number of unfair laws. Every part of life in South Africa became separated by race: schools, transportation, sports teams, restaurants, and even cemeteries. Eventually, separate "homelands" were created for black South Africans. The government ordered everyone from the same ethnic group to live in the same homeland. More than three million people were forced to move.

Houses in the homelands were crowded and dirty. They did not have indoor plumbing. Non-whites could travel outside their homeland only for work.

The laws were part of a system called *apartheid* (uh-PAR-tite), which means

"apartness." Blacks were arrested for sitting in "whites only" seats on buses or staying out past curfew.

Nelson Mandela and the ANC decided it was time to act.

5
Defiance

By 1952, Nelson had earned a diploma
and was able to practice law. He and a
friend from college opened the first black
law firm in South Africa. They represented
people who were arrested under the new
apartheid laws. Every morning, they'd find
a crowd of people waiting to see them.
They often worked late into the night.

When Nelson wasn't at the office or in court, he was working with the ANC. They had a plan called the Defiance Campaign. Nelson advised protesters to disobey laws they felt were unfair. This is called *civil disobedience.* Some black people rode "whites only" train cars. Others marched in the streets, singing songs about freedom. Some broke their curfews. They were always peaceful wherever they went. During the campaign, some ANC protesters were beaten. Many were arrested, including Nelson.

After this, the government made life even worse for non-white people. Nelson and other ANC leaders were banned from going to ANC meetings or work and had to stay in their homes.

In 1955, the ANC and other anti-apartheid groups joined forces. They held a meeting called the Congress of the People. Together, they made a list of rights they wanted, such as voting and owning property. They agreed on it and called it the Freedom Charter. On the second day of meetings, the police broke up the peaceful group.

6
Treason!

DECEMBER 5, 1956. SOWETO.
Early one morning, the police knocked on
Nelson's door. They searched his home.
They didn't find anything, but still they
arrested him for protesting apartheid.
They charged him with treason, which
meant he had supposedly betrayed
his country. All over South Africa,
156 anti-apartheid leaders were charged
with treason.

The government took four years to
prepare for the trial. Luckily, the suspects
did not have to stay in prison the whole
time. Nelson spent those years with the
ANC, preparing for the treason trial. His
law firm closed. He never saw his family.
He and his wife grew apart and divorced.

There was a bright spot for Nelson during this time. He met a young social worker named Winnie. They fell in love, got married, and had two daughters. But there was also a shocking event while they prepared for the treason trial to start. It changed everything for Nelson Mandela and the ANC.

7
Outlaw

On March 21, 1960, protests were taking place in a number of townships, which were areas where non-white people lived. When non-whites traveled outside the cities, they had to carry passbooks. Passbooks included information about their identity. Whites did not have to use passbooks.

In Sharpeville, over five thousand people gathered in a field to protest passbooks. They marched to the police station and sang songs. The songs got louder, and the police grew nervous. They thought the protesters were throwing rocks. The police shot at the crowd. Minutes later, sixty-nine people lay dead. Nearly two hundred were wounded.

People all over the country were furious. The ANC organized more marches, but the government cracked down. They ruled that groups like the ANC were against the law.

They arrested thousands of people, including Nelson. He was jailed for five months but never charged with a crime.

Nelson Mandela had had enough! He was tired of watching his people's peaceful protests end in arrests, beatings, and death. He and his friends had been fighting the treason charge for years. In the end, the judge declared them not guilty. Once

the trial was over, Nelson said goodbye to
Winnie and his daughters and went into
hiding.

Nelson started a secret branch of the
ANC. It was called Spear of the Nation.
He would be the leader. They would use
weapons and fight like an army. Their goal
was to make trouble for the government, not
hurt people. They set off bombs in power
plants and government offices at night.

The government declared Mandela an outlaw. Rewards were offered for his capture.

Nelson wore disguises to get around and only saw his family in secret. He even left South Africa to meet with foreign leaders. He was hoping to raise money for the ANC.

When he returned to South Africa, Nelson drove from one secret meeting to another. On August 5, 1962, he was driving back to Johannesburg. His car was ambushed by the police. Nelson was captured and sentenced to five years in prison.

8
One More Trial

After almost a year in prison, Nelson got bad news. ANC members were being arrested. The police discovered maps and other papers showing Spear of the Nation's plans. Nelson went on trial with his friends.

They were accused of trying to take down the government. If they were found guilty, they might be hanged!

When it was time to present their case, Nelson defended the whole group. He spoke for almost three hours. He admitted everything Spear of the Nation had done. But he did not apologize. He said, "I have cherished the ideal of a democratic and

free society in which all persons will
live together in harmony and with equal
opportunities. It is an ideal for which I
hope to live and to see realized. But . . . if
it needs be, it is an ideal for which I am
prepared to die."

Nelson and seven others were found
guilty and sentenced to life in prison.

9
Prisoner 46664

Nelson was forty-five years old when he returned to prison. This time, his friends went, too. They were sent to a prison on Robben Island. Nelson was known as Prisoner 46664. He was given a shirt, a pair of shorts, a few thin blankets, and a bucket for a toilet. His cell was eight by seven feet.

Prisoners worked long days in the quarry. They broke up rocks side by side but were not allowed to speak to each other.

The conditions were horrible. Over time, Nelson used non-violent methods to make changes. He always walked proudly in front of the guards, no matter how scared he was.

He planned work stoppages with the prisoners. Sometimes they would not eat until they were treated less harshly. It took many years, but slowly they were given better clothes and food.

While in prison, Nelson studied Afrikaans, the white minority's language. He wanted to understand the language of his enemies.

10
On the Outside

The police did not stop bothering Nelson's family even though he was in jail. They followed Winnie. They searched her home and questioned her whenever they wanted.

She could visit Nelson only twice a year. Each visit lasted half an hour. In 1969, Winnie herself was arrested, and she was held for sixteen months. Over and over again, she was questioned, arrested, abused, and banned from leaving her house.

During this time, a new generation of protesters grew up. It was harder than ever for black children to go to school. The laws became stricter. The National Party commanded schools to teach some lessons in Afrikaans. On June 16, 1976, the students of Soweto protested. They refused to go to school. They refused to take a test in a language they didn't know. So they marched through their township holding signs. Some of them threw rocks at the police. The police aimed their guns at the crowd and fired.

For days, people rioted in Soweto. More than five hundred of them died.

In prison, Nelson could not listen to the radio or read newspapers. But some of the guards gave him newspaper clippings about Winnie. And when new prisoners arrived on Robben Island, they told Nelson and his friends about the student protests.

11
Free Mandela!

People outside South Africa were shocked by what they saw on the news. Foreign companies canceled business deals with South Africa. Sports teams refused to play against South Africa's athletes. Concerts and protests were held all over the world to support Nelson Mandela. The country was going broke!

Nelson and a few friends were moved to a new prison in 1982. They'd been on Robben Island for eighteen years.

Over the next few years, Nelson met secretly with government officials. They offered him freedom if he stopped fighting apartheid using violence and told his followers to do the same. Nelson refused. He would rather stay in prison than give up his dream of equality for *all* South Africans.

A new president, F. W. de Klerk, was elected in September 1989. Nelson met with him in December, and once again he explained why apartheid must end. This president listened. Less than two months later, de Klerk lifted the ban on groups like the ANC and freed political prisoners. Nelson's prison sentence was finally over.

12
Freedom

February 11, 1990. Victor Verster Prison.
After twenty-seven years in prison,
seventy-one-year-old Nelson Mandela left
as a free man. A car drove him through
the prison gates. Nelson and Winnie got
out of the car and raised their hands to
the hundreds of people cheering. They
drove to Cape Town, where more than a
hundred thousand people waited to see
him. Celebrations were held everywhere!

Nelson knew there was still much work
to be done. In 1991, he became president
of the ANC. The fighting in the townships
and among the politicians did not stop
right away. It took a few more years and

many more meetings before all of South
Africa's political parties agreed to hold
a democratic election. But the world was
watching. In 1993, Mandela and President
de Klerk were awarded the Nobel Peace
Prize! And finally, on April 27, 1994,
more than nineteen million people voted,
including former Prisoner 46664.

Nelson Mandela served one term as president. He stepped down in 1999 and devoted the rest of his life to helping people in South Africa. He worked to educate them about AIDS. He met with foreign governments and invited them to bring their business back to South Africa.

When he wasn't traveling the world, Nelson enjoyed getting to know his many grandchildren and great-grandchildren. He died at home on December 5, 2013.